THE REMARKABLE LIFE OF KITTY MCINERNEY

How a Poor Irish Immigrant Raised 17 Children in Great Depression New York

by Christopher Prince

This book is dedicated to all the courageous men and women who made the long journey, to the Irish for their unbreakable spirit, to Kitty who forever watches over us, and to the McInerney children who keep the memories alive. May we never forget the sacrifices of those who came before us.

CONTENTS

ACKNOWLEDGEMENTS

I am tremendously grateful to the children of Kitty McInerney for all the time and support they generously provided me during the writing of this book. I am particularly thankful for Helen's unfailing memory and for the opportunity to interview Jim and Bonnie before their untimely passing. I greatly appreciate the generosity of my Irish cousins who provided such a wonderful perspective and introduced me to their great country: Anne Cadden, Hubert Kearns, Paddy O'Malley and Gerald O'Malley. I thank John Payne for his thorough and poetic recounting of Bronx history and for being a dear family friend all these years. I thank my wife, Jessica, for forever changing my life and my mother, Ginny, for truly being her mother's daughter, offering her unwavering faith and support every step of the way.

Expression

A tree can't sing when its arms are bare
But it finds its songs when the birds nest there
As a mother does when she sighs in vain
For a way to express her soul's refrain

God plants a seedling with tender care
Near a mother's heart and it blossoms there
So it isn't strange when a child, it seems,
Can express its mother's secret dreams

And many a mother on High today
Smiles down in a proud and gentle way
When she hears her child sing a song
That she carried locked in her heart so long.

by Kitty McInerney's Favorite Poet, Nick Kenny
Originally published in the New York Mirror

KNOCKS

The small village of Scotshouse nestles quietly on the north-central boundary of what is today the Republic of Ireland, just a few kilometers from the border of Northern Ireland. The town's soft, rolling hills and quiet air mask the turbulent history of the region, as political oppression, famine, and mass emigration plagued Irish society for centuries.

While the English maintained control over Irish society for nearly three centuries, the Irish Catholic majority toiled mostly as farmhands on land owned by their English masters. Despite many efforts at political reform, Irish farm laborers remained poor, overworked, and powerless.

In the mid-nineteenth century, the potato crops on which the Irish economy and diet so heavily relied suffered a catastrophic fungal disease transmitted from imported Peruvian crops. The disease spread swiftly throughout Europe. In Ireland alone, as 75% of the potato crop was destroyed, one million Irishmen died, and another two million emigrated within fifteen years. In the span of only two generations, the Irish population was cut in half.

At the depths of the Great Famine, Mary Frances "Fanny" Gibson of Scotshouse was raised Protestant Irish in nineteenth century English tradition— reserved, solemn and above all, proper. Serving as a maid, Fanny's refined manners earned her social access to the English gentry, rare for someone of her status. Her English breeding could have brought her further social advantages over her Catholic neighbors, but Fanny Gibson contradicted her very nature and violated a cardinal rule of English society: she fell in love with a Catholic. When Fanny married a Catholic farmer from nearby Cavan, she knowingly sacrificed her social status and her family, who immediately disowned her.

Unable to purchase land, Fanny Gibson and her groom, James Smith, rented a farm house on Drumbure, a townland of Scotshouse. At Drumbure, the Smiths lived the modest life of a farmer and midwife and raised a family of their own.

Patrick Smith became the oldest of Fanny and James' six children. Unlike his siblings, whom he often spoke of as uppity and snobbish, Patrick Smith was down-to-earth and displayed a vibrant sense of humor. He was also well-mannered and hard working, qualities that served him as a farmer on the nearby estate of Hilton Park, where he tended to horses and cattle.

In his early twenties, Patrick Smith married Mary Anne McCaul, a midwife and herbalist whose family owned a small farm called Knocks on the outskirts of Scotshouse. In addition to tending to farm duties on Knocks, Mary Anne delivered a number of the town's children from the parish priest's house and treated sickness with tonics she created from plants and herbs gathered along streams and rivers.

On April 26th, 1908, Patrick and Mary Anne Smith gave birth to their first child, Catherine Ellen. Kitty, as she came to be known, would never have a memory of being raised by her parents. After the birth of the Smith's second child, Minnie, and as the demands of farm life proved too great, Kitty was sent to Knocks to be raised by her maternal grandparents.

Although Kitty regularly visited her parents in town, Kitty's life with her grandparents in Knocks would define her childhood. Life on the farm was demanding. Food was scarce and everyone, including children, toiled from the break of dawn. Even schooling was a challenge. Kitty walked miles every day through the hills of Scotshouse to attend elementary school. After the sixth grade, twelve-year old Kitty was forced to abandon school and tend to Knocks full time. But she rarely complained, because beyond her love for her grandparents and devotion to her duties, Kitty found great inspiration from farm life. She often roamed the farm freely, developing a love for the outdoors and a deep fondness for animals. Even as a young girl, Kitty often defied her grandparents by sneaking eggs or skimmed milk to a hungry dog. When the day's labor was complete, Kitty recited poetry and played the accordion for her wearied uncles and grandparents. On Sundays she hiked into town to attend Catholic mass with her family, which grew to five siblings. Despite their separation, Kitty was quite fond of her parents and had assumed many of their qualities... her mother's calm, affable nature and spiritualism, her father's sense of humor and impeccable manners.

Kitty would always cherish her idyllic childhood in Knocks. But as was the inevitable fate of so many young Irishmen before her, Kitty would have no future in her beloved Ireland.

AMERICAN WAKE

In the early part of the twentieth century, Ireland suffered great bloodshed as Irish Catholics made a concerted push for self rule. In 1919, a secret organization was formed with one primary objective in mind: unequivocal independence from Great Britain. The Irish Republican Army, financed heavily by Irish Americans, fought a protracted guerilla war against British forces in Ireland, bombing police stations, convoys, and any outposts of British control. In a brutal and desperate effort to suppress the rebellion, British auxiliary forces known as the Black & Tans burned villages, executed rebels, and murdered civilians. A brief cease-fire was extinguished by months of bloody civil war. In 1922, England finally established the Irish Free State among the twenty-six counties of the South, granting financial, judicial, political and educational independence to Ireland.

Yet centuries-old problems continued to plague Ireland as a majority of its people lived and died with agriculture. As agricultural exports sagged, many young Irishmen flocked to the cities for work, but low industrial wages and the condition of urban slums made life unbearable. In the 1920s, over 20% of the population lived in inadequate, overcrowded housing. Facing little opportunity on the farms and squalid conditions in the cities, the young people of Ireland continued their mass exodus to other lands of opportunity.

For seventeen year-old Kitty Smith, circumstances were no less bleak. So when her Aunt Nelly visited from America and offered to sponsor her citizenship, Kitty reluctantly accepted. For most Irish emigrants, departure for America would be preceded by a gathering of friends and family. It was called the American wake, because so often those left behind would be saying their final goodbyes. But for Kitty, there was no American wake. Her travel plans were hastened, and neither her mother nor father was told ahead of time of her impending departure. Mary Anne hurried to Knocks just in time to say goodbye to her daughter. But Patrick, the father that Kitty so adored, was too late. By the time he got word and hurried his way down the narrow lanes to Knocks, Kitty was gone. Denied even a moment of farewell with his departing daughter, Patrick was left to weep for days.

Kitty had boarded a train for the port city of Derry on the north coast of Ireland. On December 19th, 1925, she and dozens of other poor Irish embarked the steamship Caledonia to follow generations of Irishmen across the Atlantic. As Kitty watched the Irish coast fade, her thoughts were not of her long journey or uncertain future, but of the modest life and people she was leaving behind in Scotshouse. She knew quite well, at age seventeen, she would not likely see her mother, father, or dearest grandparents ever again.

GREENHORN

The Irish began sailing to America in significant numbers by the eighteenth century. Hamstrung by English trade restrictions, mostly Protestant Irish from the North boarded ships in search of greater opportunity on the other side of the Atlantic. By the time of the American Revolution, one quarter of a million Irishmen had already immigrated to America.

After nineteenth century industrialism took hold, legions of agrarian laborers abandoned American farms in favor of factory work in the cities. Cities grew rapidly, and the mode of connecting cities and expanding trade routes became a priority. The Irish who landed on American soil found ample opportunity in factories and along canals and railroads. Irish enclaves were formed across an ever-expanding America, with Irish concentration on the Eastern seaboard in New England, New Jersey, Pennsylvania, and New York.

But after the Great Famine struck the potato fields of Ireland in the 1840s, Irish immigration to America took on a strikingly different character. The famine Irish were not the Protestant, relatively well-to-do immigrants who had assimilated seamlessly into American society for nearly a century. The new Irish immigrants were largely poor, unskilled, unfamiliar with urban life, and Catholic. These Irishmen were not welcome. Contrary to America's renown for liberty and tolerance, the famine Irish were met widely with bigotry and hatred. Many Americans came to believe that an excess of foreigners and

Catholics would destroy the fabric of a blossoming democracy. Anti-foreign and anti-Catholic mobs attacked convents and Catholic schools throughout the Northeast. Riots erupted in Philadelphia and New York. Irish Catholics were shunned by landlords and shop owners and denied work in the factories.

An unfavorable reception, coupled with immigrant loneliness and yearning for Ireland, intensified the growth of Irish slums. Filth, disease, crime, and alcoholism prevailed in the Irish ghettos. Ex-peasant Irishmen battled a debilitating sense of inferiority and yearned for respectability. But from the depths of despair, Irish immigrants found salvation in their only political capital: their escalating numbers, their unbreakable unity, and their irrevocable right to vote.

Throughout the latter half of the nineteenth century, in cities across the Northeast, Irish immigrants banded together in support of political leaders who championed their causes. Labor unions became inundated with Irishmen who ensured good paying jobs for immigrants. Numerous social groups and organizations sprang up and gave Irish immigrants a sense of belonging. The Catholic Church expanded to become a major force in representing Irish values socially and politically. By the end of the nineteenth century, the Irish had permeated American culture. Songs like "Sweet Rosie O'Grady" and "My Wild Irish Rose" became genuinely American. Irishmen like John L. Sullivan, Paddy Ryan and Gentlemen Jim Corbett dominated the vastly popular sport of boxing.

In America's pastime, John McGraw and Charles A. Comiskey built baseball empires in New York and Chicago, respectively. And the "Fighting Irish" were fast becoming the preeminent name in football.

Nowhere was the influence of the Irish immigrant more pronounced than in America's most powerful city, New York. 75% of the famine Irish landed in New York harbor, and by 1860 a quarter of New York City's population was Irish. Within a few decades, the Irish held firm control over Tammany Hall, the Democratic Party political machine that controlled much of New York politics. The rise of the Irish in New York culminated when Al Smith, the grandson of Irish immigrants, rose from the tenements of the Lower East Side to become governor of New York in the 1920s.

For the Irish immigrant who anchored in New York Harbor in the first decades of the twentieth century, no longer were prejudice, hatred and aggression there to spurn them. In their place was a new Irish-American identity, confident, proud, and irrepressible, ready to be assumed by the next greenhorn to step down from the deck of an Irish steamship.

This was the America that greeted Kitty Smith after she completed her long journey from Derry, Ireland to New York Harbor on December 28, 1925. Her life in the new country, however, had anything but an auspicious beginning. Her name had been misspelled by a crewman on the Caledonia's ship manifest. She was listed as Katie instead of Kitty, and her last name, Smith, was misspelled with a "y." As a result, she could not be properly identified by relatives. The shy, 105-pound newcomer was claimed by a Traveler's Aid and sent to the Leo Home on 23rd Street in Manhattan. The Home was supervised by an order of nuns who spoke only German. For two days, Kitty's only companion in her new country was a cat. Finally, after considerable effort, Kitty's Aunt Nellie was permitted to claim her. Nellie took Kitty to her home at 61 Bryant Street in Newark, New Jersey, and Kitty's life in America officially began.

Kitty worked for a short time as a child's nurse in Newark. Before long, she was making her way around Manhattan, assisting at a hospital and working as a maid for well-to-do families. In 1927 she began working as a domestic for the Woolseys, the family of an English doctor who resided on East 36th Street. She labored six days a week as a maid, but she was treated well and grew very fond of the family. During the summer, Kitty traveled with the Woolseys to their summer home in Cornwall, Connecticut. The rustic setting, roaming fields, kerosene lamps, and coal stove all reminded Kitty of home.

Back in the city, Kitty did everything she could to remain connected with her Irish roots. She visited family often, which now included her sister, Minnie, who immigrated in 1927. Minnie was the second-oldest Smith child. Despite their closeness in age, Kitty and Minnie were very different people. Minnie was sent as a young girl to live on Drumbure with her paternal grandmother, Fanny Gibson. Fanny's traditional English household was strict and proper, and many of Minnie's aunts who remained there were uppity and aloof. While Kitty enjoyed a childhood of roaming, laughter and warmth on Knocks, Minnie's life on Drumbure was comparatively cold and restrained. The two sisters whose lives converged thousands of miles from home had long since assumed very different personalities. Minnie would always struggle to understand her sister, especially as the circumstances of Kitty's life became increasingly complicated.

In addition to family, Kitty sought familiarity in Irish dance halls. All over New York City Irish immigrants gathered every weekend to celebrate with song and dance from the old country. Each hall hosted a dance in honor of a particular Irish county, allowing immigrants to reunite with familiar faces or meet new ones.

On one such night in 1927, a festive, nineteen year -old Kitty Smith looked across the room and locked eyes with a handsome, charming, and brash young man from County Clare. He had a rapturous look, spoke with a delightful wit, sung beautifully, and was an elegant dancer. As Kitty would come to discover, he was also... trouble.

BULL'EM MCINERNEY

Michael Joseph McInerney grew up in Kilrush, County Clare, a picturesque coastal village that sits near the mouth of the River Shannon in the southwest of Ireland. With the arrival of a railway in the late nineteenth century, combined with shipping from the Atlantic, Kilrush quickly developed into a bustling seaport and market town.

Michael was one of seven children and the son of an Irish laborer who fought for the English in the South African Boer War. From an early age, Michael McInerney displayed abundant charm and ingratiated himself throughout the village. He was a star football player, known widely as "Bull'em McInerney" for his toughness on the soccer field. He sported a reckless streak, stealing boats docked from Scattery Island and sailing around the Atlantic coast. He often found trouble in town, which led on numerous occasions to his being jailed. Much of Michael McInerney's reprobate behavior was fueled by an affliction that would plague him throughout his life: a consuming and unrelenting addiction to alcohol.

With opportunity in the villages becoming as dismal as life on the farms, Michael set out for Limerick Station and boarded a train for the port of Cobh in the South of Ireland. Years later, when he was asked the details of his trip to America, Michael would only answer, "I swam the Atlantic." In reality, Michael McInerney set sail for America on the steamship Carinthia in August of 1926 at the age of nineteen. He was received by his brother Pat at the Port of New

York and taken to 113th Street in Manhattan.

With his charm and knack for song and dance, Michael easily got work in the Irish dance halls as a waiter or bus boy. He was beloved by employers and patrons alike, but the free liquor he received as a perk of his profession would be his undoing, sending him on benders and costing him job after job.

But for one evening in 1927, Michael's intoxication was fueled not by alcohol but by the presence of a fair and engaging young woman from the Irish countryside. Kitty Smith was everything Michael McInerney yearned for: genuine, maternal and stable. As for Kitty, she could only see Michael's charm and wit through the lens of her own honest and genuine upbringing. She did not comprehend the depths of his troubles.

So the country girl from Scotshouse fell in love with the city boy from Kilrush. Before Kitty left for another trip to the Woolsey home in Connecticut, Michael, fearing the separation would doom their relationship, proposed to marry Kitty before she left. Michael McInerney and Kitty Smith married at St. Michael Church in Manhattan on January 26, 1928. Kitty didn't even tell her sister, Minnie, knowing that Minnie did not like Michael and would disapprove.

After the wedding, Kitty continued to live with the Woolseys for another year, honoring her commitment to the family. In the meantime, Michael lived with his brother John and bounced from job to job in the dance halls. Despite Prohibition, Michael was regularly getting drunk and testing his brother's patience.

In early 1929, the young couple learned that Kitty was pregnant with their first child. Shortly after, Kitty said goodbye to the Woolseys and she and Michael finally took an apartment together on 102nd Street in Manhattan. During this time, Michael settled down and took a job as a shipping clerk at Wannamakers Department Store, a position he would hold for two years—the longest tenure he would ever have at one job. Michael was here on the morning of October 19th, 1929, when Kitty went into labor. With no one around to assist her, Kitty headed for the hospital by herself, but not before dropping off laundry at the cleaners despite labor pains. She made her way to Flower Fifth Avenue Hospital on the West Side, but was turned away and told to go to her own doctor miles away in The Bronx. Kitty boarded a subway train and headed to the northern borough. Upon exiting the train, Kitty, now in advanced labor, ascended a hundred steps to reach the sidewalk, then walked a mile before reaching her doctor. Within an hour, she gave birth to a daughter, Helen Patricia McInerney.

With the birth of Helen, the McInerney family shared the optimism of an entire nation. The 1920s had been very good to America. Peace and economic expansion had fostered goodwill everywhere. The marketplace was booming. The night clubs were jostling with a roaring new sound. A burgeoning art form, motion pictures, came of age with its own kind of sound. As the nation seemed to have shed its troubled past and looked forward with boundless zeal, the McInerneys embraced a promising future with a new family in a country that was fast becoming home.

But on October 29th, 1929, just ten days after the birth of Helen McInerney, the irrepressible exuberance that defined an age came to a dramatic and conclusive halt, and the fate of the McInerneys, along with the rest of America, would be changed forever.

CRASH

By the late 1920s, New York City had grown to become the world's financial capital. The New York Stock Exchange was the largest stock market in the world. During the decade, American manufacturing reached record levels and corporate profits soared, sparking furious investor speculation. In the five years leading up to October of 1929, the Dow Jones Industrial Average increased five-fold. Stock prices ballooned as average working men and women dumped their life savings in the pursuit of overnight wealth. When investors lacked their own money to invest, banks freely loaned them money. With the market entrenched in a perpetual climb, no investment seemed too risky.

On October 29, 1929, after five days of extreme volatility and trepidation, the New York Stock Exchange plunged in an historic, dramatic fashion. The market dropped $14 billion in one day, almost five times the annual budget of the federal government. Stocks lost 89% of their peak value in three years. Over the next decade, more than 9,000 banks failed, costing Americans $140 billion in deposits. Prices and incomes were slashed in half, while unemployment rose to over 25%.

The panic and hysteria of the stock market crash was slowly replaced by the languor of wide scale poverty and depression. Men thronged the streets in search of scant jobs while their wives endured interminable lines for government-supplied food rations. Makeshift, squalid villages of the homeless poor, pejoratively named "Hooverville" (after the U.S. president), cropped up in cities across America. Millions of Americans battled hunger and starvation on a daily basis. Suicide was all too common. While civic leaders desperately tried to get a handle on the growing humanitarian crisis, average Americans were left to fend for themselves.

The young McInerney family began its life together in these most turbulent of times. Shortly after Helen was born, Michael lost his job at Wannamaker's. Although jobs were scarce, Michael's charm and sense of humor always seemed to open the door for work, though his alcoholism affected Michael's willingness and ability to sustain work for very long. On many occasions, he spent his paycheck on liquor and left Kitty with nothing. Before long, the family could no longer afford to live in Manhattan. The McInerneys were forced to move to a northern borough, a former rustic backcountry that was fast becoming the seat of culture, diversity and opportunity for the working class American immigrant.

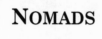

NOMADS

The Bronx is the only borough of New York City situated on the American mainland. Formerly a wilderness of forests, meadows, and streams inhabited by various Indian tribes, The Bronx was settled by the Dutch in the seventeenth century. Marginally separated from upper Manhattan by the narrow Harlem River, The Bronx quickly became a convenient destination for migrants seeking to escape the overcrowding and high costs of Manhattan.

The Irish first came to the Bronx in the mid nineteenth century as gangs of laborers who constructed the New York and Harlem Railroad, the Hudson River Railroad and the High Bridge. Their backbreaking and highly dangerous work inspired the saying that American railroads had "an Irishman buried under every tie." Later, Irish migrants filled the newly-built Bronx factories or commuted to jobs in Manhattan. They settled their families in neat wooden frame houses within the Bronx neighborhoods of Mott Haven, Melrose, and Highbridge, where they tended to pigs, cows and chickens and cultivated vegetable gardens in the backyards.

Other waves of immigration in the early twentieth century brought Italians, Germans, and Eastern European Jews to the Bronx. At the same time, Manhattan subway lines extended north and attracted furious development. Brick walk-ups sprouted seemingly overnight, lining street after street, providing rental housing to the mostly working class residents and transforming the Bronx into its own city. By the late 1920s, the Bronx was booming with over 1.2 million people, mostly first- and second-generation immigrants who worked as carpenters, brick masons, house painters, tailors, garment makers, store clerks, small shop owners, and salesmen.

The Bronx community of the 1930s was self-sustaining for a majority of its residents, complete with new apartment houses, tree-lined streets, spacious public parks, good schools and ample shops. Social life blossomed on stoops and in apartment courtyards, weaving a tight fabric of community life. Millions of Americans came to know the Bronx through "The Rise of the Goldbergs," a popular radio and, later, television show depicting the lives of a Jewish family from the Bronx.

The Bronx that greeted Michael, Kitty and Helen McInerney in 1930 was a hopeful place, but one that could not escape the growing despair of the age. Despite its charms, The Bronx was hit hard by the Depression. A Hooverville emerged on the Harlem River near Highbridge. New construction dropped 75% from its 1920s highs. Evictions tripled throughout the city. In such an environment, the McInerneys home life was anything but stable. After initially moving to 137th Street in the Irish neighborhood of Mott Haven, poverty, a growing family, and Michael's alcoholism forced the family to uproot time after time.

After a short, unpleasant stay at 137th Street, the family moved to the top floor at 140th. Despite Prohibition, an illegal "still" was run across the hall. The men drank all day and Michael gladly joined them. Mary was born in April of 1931 and the family moved to 141st Street.

By the time Anna was born in March in 1933, the nation had reached the depths of depression. There was no work. Kitty was lucky to get milk from Gold Medal Farms and bread from a Jewish bakery. Welfare coupons helped to put food on the table, but barely enough to feed a growing family. Due to complications in delivering Anna, Kitty was forced to stay in the hospital for a number of days. Her sister Minnie checked in on the children at home and found Michael drunk with his friends and thirty-two small bottles of liquor on the fire escape. The utilities had been shut off. Minnie gave Michael the money to pay the utilities, but he used it for liquor. So she took Helen and Mary to Maggie McNamara's, a relative of Michael's through marriage. When Kitty arrived home, the utilities were still off, forcing her to heat Anna's bottle on the radiator.

Shortly after, Kitty took a janitor's job just to survive. The family moved to a Jackson Avenue basement apartment with no bathroom, only a shared toilet in the coal bin. Kitty shoveled coal and cleaned the apartment house, all with very little help from Michael.

Kitty delivered her first son, Jackie, in June of 1934 while Michael and a few drinking buddies gathered around the radio in the next room to listen to a boxing match. It was at this time that Kitty befriended a neighboring Irish family, the McEntees, who for many years provided desperately needed support to the McInerneys in the form of money, food, and help during child labor.

The McInerneys moved again in July of 1935 to a Dawson Street apartment with two small bedrooms and only one dresser for all the children to share. To earn free rent and ten dollars a month, Kitty cleaned the entire two-building property, polishing doorknobs, scrubbing the stoop, and shoveling coal into the furnaces—a job that began at five a.m. daily. At the same time, Kitty cared for all her children and washed clothes and linens by hand. By the time Kitty finished her household chores, she was lucky to get to bed by one or two in the morning. Neighbors were often awakened by the sound of the laundry line pulley squeaking during the wee hours of the morning, inspiring one neighbor to offer Kitty a gift of oil to halt the noise.

Despite the cramped space, Kitty regularly took in Michael's homeless drinking buddies for the night and let them sleep in the basement. If Kitty had food, she would feed them. She always showed Michael's alcoholic friends care and kindness and never spoke unkindly about them.

Theresa was born in October of 1935. Shortly afterwards, Michael had an affair with an Irish neighbor woman who lived with her husband and children on the top floor. Kitty scolded Michael and never spoke to the woman again. Michael, however, remained close friends with the woman's husband.

Eileen was born a year later, in January of 1937. The neighbors became intolerant of Kitty's growing family and Michael's binge drinking, and the Board of Health came and forced the family to move in the January cold and snow. After a few days' search, the McInerneys landed an apartment at 160th and Tinton Avenue, but that was soon demolished to make way for a new building.

It was on to 158th Street, where, in May of 1938, Kitty went into labor and walked a mile to get help. She delivered Paddy as Michael got drunk in a local bar. The following day, seven year-old Mary returned home and reported that Helen, Kitty's oldest child, had died. After several minutes of panic, it was discovered that Helen had been struck by a car on Westchester Avenue and thrown into a pillar. Despite injuries that restricted her to bed for four days, Helen actually lived.

When the owner of the 158th street building claimed the apartment for himself, the McInerneys moved to Avenue St. John. A moving foundation forced them to East 152nd Street, where Eugene was born in October of 1939. Before his first birthday, Gene battled pneumonia twice and suffered a case of measles. Doctors were forced to treat Gene with sulfur, which would save his life but limit him mentally as he got older. Climbing four floors at East 152nd proved to be unbearable, so after a few short moves the family landed at Trinity Avenue, where Margaret was born in December of 1940. Kitty's condition was deteriorating, having suffered a bout of heart palpitations during pregnancy. She was advised by doctors not to have any more children.

Late one Christmas Eve, Helen, hearing the familiar sound of a squeaking laundry pulley, stepped into the cold midnight air. As the new Christmas morning approached, Helen found Kitty hanging laundry in the darkness. It didn't take long for Helen to discover that her mother was crying. News had just come in from Ireland. Ellen McCaul, the woman who raised Kitty on the small farm in Knocks, the loving grandmother Kitty hadn't seen since leaving for the train to Derry, had died. Time would soon claim Kitty's mother and father too. It was here, in the dark Christmas morning, wet clothes hanging on a drooping line, where Kitty finally understood everything she had sacrificed in coming to America.

I Have Children for Those Who Can't

In the first decade of the Great Depression, Kitty McInerney had given birth to nine children. She had moved her family fifteen times in a desperate pilgrimage of survival while working herself to exhaustion twenty hours a day. Kitty's struggle would have been brutal enough even with a supportive husband. But Michael was anything but supportive, and his worsening alcoholism plagued Kitty at every turn. Michael rarely worked, and when he did, he horded his paychecks to buy liquor. During drunken rages, Michael was verbally abusive towards Kitty. When short on money and in need of a fix, Michael stole virtually anything with resale value: coal from the furnace Kitty fed every morning, a pair of drapes from Kitty's window, shoes and pants from a drunk, unconscious friend, a chair from a funeral parlor, a neighbor's cat. "I wish I went down with the Caledonia," Kitty would say, referring to the steamship that had brought her to America and later sank.

As 1940 came to a close, the family was extremely poor and welfare was limited. With the holidays approaching, they were unable to afford a Christmas tree. The McInerney children scoured through tree lots and gathered broken branches in order to build their own makeshift tree. If it weren't for the McEntees, who arrived on Christmas morning with small gifts of jacks and balls, there would have been no Christmas.

Yet Kitty persisted through the turmoil and chaos. Despite doctors' warnings, she continued to have children. With the nation was now at war and many of the country's mothers losing their children in battle, Kitty seemed ordained to bring forth new life. A move to Cauldwell Avenue was followed by the birth of two more children, Bonnie in 1942 and Tommy in 1943. Rarely did Kitty announce a pregnancy. The children learned to expect a new member of the family when they saw Kitty converting a dresser drawer into a baby bed. Furthermore, Kitty never discussed sexuality with any of her children, including daughters. On one occasion Helen asked Kitty where babies came from. Kitty responded tersely, "There's a place," then stormed out of the room.

By this point, neighbors were shocked and in some cases disdainful of Kitty for having more children. Even Kitty's own sister, Minnie, seldom visited because she could not understand why Kitty remained with Michael and had so many children. Kitty's only response: "I have children for those who can't." In truth, Kitty was a devout Catholic and did not believe in divorcing a man to whom she had committed her life, regardless of his sickness, nor did she believe in artificially preventing what she believed God had planned for her. Despite the burdens, Kitty was never happier than when she was pregnant or caring for an infant.

But having so many children came with an emotional price. Kitty had neither the time nor resources to adequately address Michael's alcoholism. Her growing battles with Michael during his drunken rages was a source of horror and conflict for the children. Once the victim of Michael's verbal abuse, Kitty gradually became more empowered, responding to his apathy or aggression with blows of her own. One night, she threw him down a flight of stairs. On another, she doused him with kerosene and stormed the house in search of a match. But she always forgave him and catered to him during hangovers, and never did she allow the children to criticize him. What's more, Kitty did not tolerate conflict among any of her children, going so far as tearing a blouse in half once it became the object of dispute. Kitty's policy of peace was necessary to maintain order in an overburdened, impoverished home, but it cost her children the valuable experience of resolving disputes.

In August of 1944, after a decade and a half of tumultuous, nomadic instability, the McInerneys took residence at a railroad-style apartment on Tinton Avenue near the corner of 152nd Street. Tinton Avenue, named after Tintern Abbey in Wales, was a street not unlike many others winding through the Bronx: a nearby grocery and Jewish deli on the corner, a Catholic Church and school next door, and scores of the working poor chatting on stoops all throughout the neighborhood. Neither was the Tinton apartment exceptional in any way. At four and half bedrooms and one bathroom, it was no more adequate to accommodate the expanding McInerney clan that the numerous flats that preceded it. Nonethe-

less, 663 Tinton Avenue brought with it an unprece-
dented stability. Over the next year, thousands of
soldiers returned home, filling up available housing
and making apartment hopping in the landlocked
Bronx much more difficult. As a result, Tinton Avenue would become home to the McInerneys for the
next fifteen years.

**Kitty's Maternal Grandmother,
Ellen McCaul**

**Kitty's Paternal Grandmother,
Fanny Gibson**

**Kitty's Sister & Mother,
Tessie and Mary Anne Smith**

Tessie and Kitty's Father, Patrick Smith

Kitty (right), Minnie (Center) and siblings in Ireland

Kitty in Connecticut

Minnie & Kitty in New York

Michael (front) and friend in New York

Minnie (right)
holding baby Helen

Mary and Helen

Anna

Paddy, Tommy & John on Tinton Avenue

Terry

Eileen

Kitty & Paddy

Gene & Friend

Margaret

Bonnie

Tommy

Gerry

Ginny

Jimmy & Gerard

Susan

Kevin

Michael & Kitty in Tinton Avenue Apartment

Kitty & Michael Dancing

Mary in Park

Helen (center) with McInerney Children

Schoolchildren Walking down Tinton Avenue

McInerney Children on Couch

LIFE ON A STOOP

After the move to Tinton Avenue, the McInerney family functioned with strict order and discipline. Kitty continued to manage a mountain of chores with the efficiency of a small army. Helen helped care for the children while Mary mastered the art of housecleaning. From the age of eight, John worked stocking shelves at Hoffman's Grocery to help put food on the table. The other children performed their roles dutifully. Everyone knew their routine, from dressing, to eating, to bathing, to going to bed. Remarkably, Kitty maintained order not by pounding an iron fist but through a calm, quiet conviction. Kitty inspired in her children a commitment to family and to the cause of survival. Visitors often remarked how impeccably clean, ordered and quiet the McInerney home was, especially considering their family size and dire poverty.

The pride Kitty took in maintaining a home extended to how her children presented themselves in public. Kitty and the children regularly tended to cleaning and ironing clothes and polishing shoes. Even if they were poor, Kitty always labored to preserve her children's dignity. In return, every one of Kitty's children shared a grand fear of causing their mother anguish. For that reason, the McInerney children rarely caused trouble.

Despite her own ample responsibilties, Kitty maintained a profound sense of grace and courtesy. She always took time to welcome visitors with a cup of tea and a sympathetic ear. Minnie visited from time to time, delighting the children with pastries and cake from Cushman's Bakery. Kitty was appreciated by so many because of her willingness to unburden others of their troubles without casting judgment on them.

Having settled for the first time as a family, the McInerneys were able to immerse themselves in the rich community life of the 1940s Bronx. The only bearable aspect of poverty was that neighbors were poor too and knowing that everyone shared their pain. The social bonds that formed out of collective despair united the community in a mission of survival. The communal expression that arose from those bonds evinced the resiliency and spirit of the Bronx people.

Community life for most of the neighborhood revolved around the Catholic Church. St. Anselm's Church and School resided next door to the McInerneys, and most of the McInerney children attended school there. Children daily descended from apartment stoops around the neighborhood and paraded up Tinton Avenue to the school grounds, filling the morning air with shouts and laughter. Mobs of parishioners filed through the church doors for mass on Sundays and holy days, or to celebrate a wedding or bid farewell to a loved one. The highlight of spring featured a First Communion procession down Tinton Avenue, followed by graduating eighth-graders in the early summer. Boys played pool, ping pong or boxing in the school recreation room and joined girls at church dances on Friday nights. Priests walked the neighborhood, mingling with parishioners and keeping the children out of trouble. Nuns sold carnations outside the church every May to celebrate motherhood.

Beyond the church grounds boys played in the streets—games like stick ball, hand ball, kick the can, pitching pennies, Johnny on the pony, and marbles. Girls played jacks, hopscotch and jump rope. Kids raised pigeons or flew kites on rooftops and raced gleefully through alleys and courtyards. Adults congregated and watched over the neighborhood from stoops and fire escapes. In the summer, kids opened fire hydrants or flocked to the sprinklers and wading ponds of nearby St. Mary's Park for relief from the sweltering heat. They rented bikes for 25 cents, jumped on a mobile merry-go-round for a few pennies, and sat on blanketed fire escapes after sundown to unwind in the cool night air. Villagers traversed the borough on trolleys for a nickel and children hitched on the back for a free ride. The downtrodden sang in courtyards and alleys for coins and bottle caps.

Saturdays were scored by sounds of the Metropolitan Opera streaming from radios and reverberating through windows and alleyways. Holidays lured block parties and parades to crowd the Bronx thoroughfares. The carnival set up once or twice a year by Jackson Avenue station, casting a nightly glow over the South Bronx. Small shops lined the sidewalks and thrived on abundant foot traffic. Westchester Avenue from Wales to 152nd featured Dolan's Irish Food Store, Olympia Florist, Cushman's Bakery, an ice cream parlor, a drugstore, a Jewish baker, a candy store and two newsstands.

Many shop owners offered store credit to poor families like the McInerneys in need of bread, milk or meat for their children. Other neighbors and friends offered support when they could, providing small loans or passing along used clothing to needy families. On many occasions, Kitty and the McInerney children were the recipients of such generosity.

For a few weeks every summer, thousands of New York's poor children, including many McInerneys, were given a respite from the strains of poverty and city life through the New York Herald-Tribune Fresh Air Fund. Wealthy families welcomed poor children into their summer homes in Upstate New York and Connecticut, providing the underprivileged a rare experience to roam the rolling mountains and lush fields outside the Great City.

The daughter of one Fresh Air family from Maine took a liking to Mary McInerney and arranged to have a washing machine delivered to Kitty for Christmas in 1943. Kitty was overcome. If not for the compassion and generosity of the Bronx community, it's hard to imagine how families like the McInerneys would have survived. And with each passing year, it became harder to imagine the South Bronx without the McInerneys. In a span of four and a half years, Kitty brought four more children into the family:

Gerry in 1945, Ginny in 1946, Jimmy in 1948, and Gerard in 1949. Kitty, Michael and fifteen children now lived under one roof. And after Gene and Tommy accidentally caused a small fire in the storage room in 1948, the Tinton apartment was without two front rooms.

Due to Michael's inability to maintain a job, the welfare office was now making regular visits to Tinton Avenue. Michael was summoned to court, and when he failed to sway the judge with his usual charm, Michael was sentenced to six months in Riker's Island Jail just off the east coast of the Bronx. Michael worked for five months in prison, earning one dollar a day, and was released a month early for good behavior. On the day of his release, he returned home to Tinton Avenue singing. He took a bath, dressed himself neatly, then disappeared for three days on a drunken bender, blowing the entire $150 he earned in jail. Shortly after, Michael was sentenced to another six months in Rockland State Mental Hospital for alcohol rehab.

With the number of children now ballooning into the teens and Michael debilitated by alcoholism, Kitty's unbreakable determination succumbed to fear and uncertainty. She continued to suffer from a chronic nervous condition that had plagued her for years. Little did anyone realize, Kitty was quietly suffering a nervous breakdown.

FAITH

With her husband confined to a mental hospital and barely enough money to put food on the table, Kitty McInerney walked a familiar path to visit an old friend. St. Gerard at Immaculate Conception Church had comforted Kitty during many times of trouble. She prayed for guidance, for intervention, for the strength to spare her children of utter despair and hopelessness.

Kitty's capacity to manage her unique burden went beyond sheer will. Kitty was a woman of profound faith, a faith that God would endow her with the courage to persevere, a faith that she did not take up her cross alone.

Kitty's faith was the bedrock of the McInerney family experience. All of Kitty's children attended Catholic school and went to Church on Sundays at St. Anselm. Kitty spent Saturday nights polishing her children's shoes and washing the laces for the next day's service. The heels may have been crooked or broken, but the shoes were always clean. The Tinton apartment was adorned with religious artifacts: rosaries, a portrait of Jesus, a crucifix, statues of Mary, St. Anne, and the Sacred Heart. On many nights Kitty and the children knelt down to recite the rosary, especially during the month of May. Kitty often prayed at the window in the front room and attended novenas on a regular basis. She kept a prayer book nearby stuffed with people and causes she wished to pray for. Kitty believed that God hadn't given her anything she couldn't handle and that everything happens according to God's will.   And it was this faith, beyond anything else, which Kitty instilled in her children.

So even in the darkest of times, kneeling before St. Gerard at Immaculate Conception, praying for intervention, Kitty believed in her heart that God was already working to deliver her children from despair.

TIME OF TRANSITION

Michael McInerney returned home from the state hospital in early 1948 with two years of probation. Under the threat of additional jail time, he would not touch a drop of liquor for the next two years. Now on the wagon, Michael headed back to work. He got a union job with the Local 32B doing maintenance in upscale apartments in Manhattan. He charmed the landladies and earned decent money, but he often held back most of his paycheck from Kitty in order to attend prize fights at Madison Square Garden, buy a good meal, or go to the movies. He brought Gene to work with him on a number of occasions. Michael often slept in the basement while Gene ran the elevator and picked up the garbage.

Kitty was so thankful Michael was working and not drinking that she catered to him daily, preparing his breakfast and packing his lunch, and sending the kids to the market to buy ice cream for his milk-shakes.

One morning while Kitty was pregnant with Gerard, the basement began to flood. Kitty, who earned just enough for rent working as the building superintendent, headed to the basement with a wire hanger and poked the sewers in an effort to unclog the drain. She accidentally punctured her ankle, drawing blood. The wound became infected and ul-cerated. One summer day in 1949 her ankle rup-tured, sending blood all over the floor. Helen's boy-friend, George Vaughn, carried Kitty down two flights of stairs and took her to the hospital. Despite the pain, Kitty returned home and continued her tireless chores. Because she was never able to properly rest, Kitty labored in pain for the next decade before her injury was finally able to heal.

Kitty delivered Gerard in August of 1949. The summer had been rough on the McInerneys. Kitty spent the final stages of her fifteenth pregnancy suffering immensely from her ankle injury. Mary graduated high school in June and was off working in the Adirondacks and in Maine for the family she met during the Fresh Air Fund. Mary sent back all the money she made, but Kitty and Helen missed her presence around the home. Michael slept all day and worked at night, so his presence in the household was limited. And Helen, still weak and exhausted after a bout of hepatitis, was forced to quit her job in order to help take care of the children.

1949 was a time of profound transition in the life of the McInerneys. Helen had devoted her entire childhood to her mother and younger siblings. But Helen was now a woman, and what's more, she had found love. In a few short months she would begin a life and a family of her own. When Helen married George Vaughn in April of 1950, Kitty wept for what she thought would be a very hard life for Helen. Kitty gave Helen a cedar chest as a wedding gift, and as Helen carried the chest away, Kitty openly worried that Helen was carrying her own coffin out the door.

With Helen's departure, Kitty worried not only for Helen but for the future of the fourteen children who

were saying goodbye to their big sister, their care-
taker, their mother's best friend. At the same time,
Michael's probation ended, and he immediately returned to drinking and not working. In times past,
this would have signaled a return to chaos and instability—but times were changing. Michael's power to
threaten family survival was about to come to an end.

AWAKENINGS

Mary McInerney drifted through early childhood in a kind of haze. As the second-eldest of Kitty's children, she witnessed as much despair and hardship as anyone. But as a young girl, she always managed to maintain her distance from the chaos of depression and an alcohol-ravaged home life. She made quick escape to the plantations of the Deep South, the grand ballrooms of New York's finest hotels, and the palm tree-lined boulevards of Hollywood. Like so many other children of the Depression era, Mary McInerney lived an alternate life in the balcony of a movie theater. From the dark, cavernous cinemas of New York City, Mary experienced a world of carefree opulence, where poverty and alcoholism were unheard of and life's problems always had a speedy resolution. For several hours on a Saturday afternoon, hers was the world of Garbo, Gable, Hepburn, Cooper, Tracy, Stanwyck, and Garson. Whenever she could spare a nickel, either from working an odd job or Kitty selling a stack of used clothing by the pound, Mary was at the movies. And even when she wasn't there, the elegant dialogue and ethereal music of 1930s and '40s cinema played quietly in the background of her mind, quieting the alcoholic ravings of her father and softening the pangs of poverty.

As the McInerneys began to settle into Tinton Avenue, Mary slowly emerged from the fog of early childhood. Now entering her teenage years, Mary was awakening to the harsh realities of survival. Her father was a broken and diseased man. Her mother was being crushed by the weight of insurmountable responsibility. Her older sister, Helen, had surrendered the gaiety of childhood to help raise her siblings and bring solace and comfort to her mother. Mary was also becoming aware of how others regarded a family with so many children and so few means. Still just a girl, Mary vowed to never let her family succumb to the prevailing stereotype. She began to take charge of the household, working tirelessly around the apartment, delegating responsibilities to her younger siblings, providing desperately needed support to Kitty.

Mary also assumed another critical role: that of protector. One evening, not long after the move to Tinton Avenue, Michael walked through the door stinking of liquor. As he so often did, he began to harangue the children, particularly the boys, with his drunken ranting. But before Michael could impose himself physically on anyone, a fourteen year-old Mary stood toe to toe with her volatile father, matching him shout for shout, threat for threat, until finally Michael realized he had finally met his match. He backed down. Mary knew she had won, and the experience of empowerment would change her forever. Never again would she cower to her father's aggression or allow his behavior to go unchecked. Little did anyone know, but as of this moment, the seeds of the family's fate had been sewn with the awakening of Mary McInerney.

Mary returned from her job in Maine in December

of 1949, determined to finally get the family off of welfare. Years of watching movies had given rise to idealism and an unbreakable optimism for a better life. She took a job at Metropolitan Life Insurance to help support the family. Whenever Michael failed to turn over a paycheck or welfare money came up short, Mary ensured that food was on the table, the children had clothing for school, and the family was able to get medical care. When she could spare a few nickels, Mary took her younger siblings to the five-and-dime for candy and then onto the movies for a carefree afternoon. She was also a disciplinarian, making sure the children minded their chores and sweeping through the streets at night if anyone was late coming home.

Kitty's other children worked and contributed money to the household as soon as they were able. Yet, as was common for the age, most of the McInerneys married and started their families shortly after high school. Helen, having married a year earlier, gave birth to Lynn in March of 1951, the first of what would become forty-five grandchildren to Kitty. Not to be outdone, Kitty gave birth to her sixteenth child, Susan, in November of the same year. Jackie married in March of 1953, followed by Anna seven months later. Paddy entered the Navy in 1955 as a weeping Kitty watched him walk out of view down Tinton Avenue and into adulthood.

By August of 1955, Kitty had lived forty-seven years, and it had been four years since she gave birth to her last child, Susan. After years of wear and tear to her body, Kitty was starting to erode physically. She continued to bleed from fibroid tumors diagnosed ten years earlier and ended up bedridden. In time, the bleeding became so severe that Kitty was taken on a stretcher to seek medical help. Concerned about her age and the risks of further pregnancies, doctors recommended a hysterectomy, which Kitty scheduled for August 15th, the Feast of the Assumption. The night before surgery, while Kitty packed for the hospital, the phone rang. Kitty answered. "Oh my God," she exclaimed, then launched into prayer. There would be no hysterectomy. Kitty was pregnant with her seventeenth child.

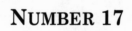

NUMBER 17

Forty-seven year-old Kitty McInerney went into labor in early December of 1955. Immediately there was trouble. Her blood pressure rose precipitously. Her face swelled. Doctors diagnosed Kitty with severe toxemia, a life-threatening condition. Moments before an emergency c-section was to be performed, a priest was summoned to minister Kitty her last rites. She was dying. A frightened Michael telephoned Helen to report the dire news. Helen almost sank to the floor. Mary was despondent and terrified. Most of the family, however, was unaware that their mother was fighting for her life.

On December 7th, Kitty delivered a healthy boy. Kevin was the seventeenth child of Kitty and Michael McInerney, and by now the community was taking notice. The Bronx Home News sent a reporter to Tinton Avenue to cover Kevin's birth. As he prepared to snap a picture of the family, Mary arrived home and immediately protested. She told him that he was free to print the story, but she did not want her siblings to appear in the public eye as desperate orphans. The Bronx Home News ran the story without a picture. Moved by the article, many people in the community assisted with clothing or whatever they could spare.

Despite a successful birth, Kitty continued to struggle for her life in the hospital. She feared not so much for herself, but for how her newborn and many young children at home would survive without her. Yet through many days of quiet reflection and prayer, Kitty slowly regained her health. After ten days in the hospital, Kitty was permitted to return home, where she was greeted by a relieved, welcoming family.

Within months of giving birth to Kevin, Kitty had a hysterectomy, ending twenty-five years of childbearing. Kitty transitioned into the next phase of her life as the world around her transitioned too. The place the McInerneys called home—the streets, the borough, the Great City—was changing decisively and dramatically. Block by block, house by house, family by family, the community was slowly disappearing. Kitty McInerney may have survived, but she could no longer hide from the fact that her city was dying.

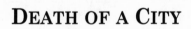

DEATH OF A CITY

Even to the youngest McInerney children, the South Bronx of the late 1950s was a much different place. Graffiti stained the stoops and shop windows. Knife fights erupted in alleyways. Trash sullied the gutter. Shops closed and longtime neighbors moved away. As the community slowly degraded, blame was commonly laid at the feet of New York's newest residents: the impoverished, poorly educated, often unskilled Puerto Rican immigrants. In reality, the decline of the South Bronx and neighborhoods across New York City was the product of perhaps the greatest political calamity of twentieth century America. Ironically, the face of that calamity was one of the most celebrated men in New York City history.

Perhaps the most striking fact about Robert Moses was that he never learned to drive a car. The German-Jewish son of a financially successful father and politically activist mother, Moses devoted a great deal of his public life to the automobile. Though a Republican, Moses rose to power in the 1920s as an aide to the affable and wildly popular Democratic Governor of New York, Al Smith. Through his vast knowledge of law and its loopholes, Moses was able to push through legislation that enabled him to hold city and state government positions simultaneously. Widely known as the city's preeminent urban planner, Moses led the construction of numerous beaches, parks and playgrounds across New York, as well as the roads and highways that led to them. In stark contrast to New York City politicians who were reviled as incompetent and corrupt, Moses was a model of efficiency and quickly gained the reputation as someone who could get the job done.

Despite a failed run for governor in 1932, Moses' popularity and reputation as the champion of the common man swelled. Whenever a mother saw her child's smiling face on a playground swing set, or teenagers romped elatedly around a public pool on a hot summer day, or a family enjoyed a few hours away from the bustling city on a tranquil Long Island Beach, often they had Robert Moses to thank for it.

Consumed with his achievements, the public and the press largely ignored the disturbing aspects of Robert Moses' methods, and in doing so failed to address his destructive vision for New York City before it was too late. When Moses built highways to his beaches, he circumvented land owned by the wealthy while dividing and destroying land owned by modest farmers. He intentionally built low overpasses that made bus travel impossible, thus excluding lower income and minority families from traveling to his white, middle-class dominated beaches. To the same end, he halted any efforts to add rail lines to his expansive highways. Although he built hundreds of parks and playgrounds around New York, very few were located in minority neighborhoods. He ordered public pools in his parks to be kept at a lower temperature because he believed it would discourage blacks from swimming in them. He provided special privileges and kickbacks to everyone he needed on his side: construction firms, investment banks, insurance companies, labor unions, real-estate developers and politicians from both major political parties. And at every turn, he overwhelmed anyone who dared to oppose him with threats and public humiliation.

As the years passed, Robert Moses, despite never holding elected office, was able to use his unwavering popularity, his reputation as a great builder, his vast knowledge of law, his underhanded deals, and his methods of intimidation to amass greater and greater power. At one point, he held twelve separate titles and had over 40,000 people working for him. As commissioner of the Triborough Bridge Authority, Moses was empowered to build bridges and interconnecting roads and highways using billions in public funds, without having to answer to a single citizen or elected politician. He plowed through thriving neighborhoods around New York City to extend his freeway system and construct on-ramps to bridges. His projects like the Cross-Bronx Expressway destroyed communities and displaced tens of thousands of families, yet the city's politicians and citizens had little power to stop Moses because they didn't control the purse strings.

Moses' vision of the new American city was unequivocal: cities were meant for cars, not people. And anyone who was unable or unwilling to use an automobile was pushed aside. Moses built mile after mile of freeway to encourage a mass exodus from the city of mostly white, middle-class families who were rapidly taking up residence in the distant suburbs. Moses diverted billions away from public transportation and infrastructure, despite the fact that automobile transportation was proving to be inefficient and destructive to community life. Within days of Moses opening a new bridge or highway, cars were jammed trying to exploit the new route. Not only were urban communities ripped apart by the new construction, new suburban neighborhoods built for cars were devoid of pedestrian convenience, depriving the suburbs of rich, village-like community life.

Robert Moses' master plan of reshaping New York coincided with a housing boom that followed World War II. During this period of what was to be called "Urban Renewal," the practice of redlining became commonplace. Redlining was a form of legalized mortgage discrimination in which governments and banks refused to invest money in homes and businesses in predominantly low-income and minority neighborhoods. While home builders flocked to areas of wide-open cheap land in Queens, Long Island and New Jersey, neighborhoods like the South Bronx were left to decay.

As money and resources shifted out of the highway -wrecked city and into the sprawling suburbs, Robert Moses was handed control of the very problem he helped create—what to do with the thousands of poor and minority families displaced by urban renewal. For those who remained in places like Harlem and the Bronx, Moses had a much different vision; he would corral these lower class leftovers into giant holding cells and keep them out of the path of urban progress. After obliterating their homes, shops and communities with his freeways, Moses injected billions in federal and state money into the construction of what would become the emblem of modern urban decline: the housing project. Moses built scores of these massive sterile skyscrapers around New York City. In a decade and a half, Moses erected 28,000 apartment units on hundreds of acres. In clearing the land for his high-rises, he often destroyed as many housing units as he built. Unlike the neighborhoods that preceded them, housing projects bore no sense of community—monotonous and barren architecture, no stoops to socialize, no corner shops, no place for mothers to watch their children playing below. Housing projects crushed nearly every aspect of village life, and in the process scared off nearly everyone capable of getting out.

But for many people living in the declining areas of New York City, there was no way out. Southern blacks had been migrating to New York since well before World War II, and their numbers nearly doubled after the war to 800,000. They sought factory work when cotton fields began to automate. Right on their heels were the Puerto Ricans, who had been granted US citizenship in 1917. In the 1940s and '50s, tens of thousands of Puerto Ricans each year fled to New York in hopes of economic opportunity in factories and shipyards. But for both blacks and Puerto Ricans, the economic landscape of New York had drastically changed since the last wave of immigrants. Low -skilled jobs were relocating to other cities and states or disappearing altogether due to technological advancements, and the few jobs that remained were closely guarded by mostly white union workers. With little economic opportunity, blacks and Puerto Ricans became mired in poverty. Crime and overcrowding plagued their neighborhoods. As whites moved out to the suburbs, blacks and Puerto Ricans snatched up their old apartments. Often Puerto Ricans lived several families to a flat, frequently without utilities. Redlining made it impossible to get loans, so they were incapable of opening businesses or buying property. And when Robert Moses and the champions of urban renewal plowed highways through their neighborhoods and demolished their homes, it was primarily the blacks and Puerto Ricans who were exiled to housing projects and virtually forgotten by the rest of the city.

As the 1950s came to a close, Kitty McInerney and most of her seventeen children found themselves in the path of Robert Moses and his wrecking ball of urban renewal. In late 1959, the McInerneys received notice that their Tinton Avenue walk-up, their home of the last fifteen years, their beacon of stability through three turbulent decades in the Bronx, was to be demolished along with most of the apartments in the neighborhood. Within weeks the McInerney children found themselves alone, walking home from school and up the empty stoop into their condemned home. The other families had moved. Except for the activity around St. Anselm School and Church, Tinton Avenue was a ghost town. No girls jumping rope or boys playing Johnny-on-the-pony. No mothers hanging laundry on the fire escapes. No fathers stepping off the train. No neighbors waving as they walked under an open window. No church processions or holiday parades. No bakeries, five-and-dimes or corner drug stores. No neighborhood. No community. No future. Only memories.

Kitty McInerney was the last to pack up her family and leave Tinton Avenue. But even after moving her family to what seemed worlds away—Walton Avenue near the Grand Concourse—Kitty still made the three-mile trek back to 663 Tinton Avenue. As she had done religiously for the last fifteen years, she swept the stairs and hallway and polished the handrails. Often asked why she continued to clean an abandoned, condemned building, Kitty responded, "I want to make it clean for the next tenant." Even under the shadow of a wrecking ball, Kitty flashed the same iron will, refusal to surrender, and stubbornness that had vaulted her through seventeen pregnancies, a near death experience, and decades of seemingly boundless turmoil.

But even the unbreakable Kitty McInerney was capable of recognizing defeat. As the old Bronx crumbled around her, Kitty was met with old, familiar calling. The same winds which decades ago blew her three thousand miles from her childhood home were swirling once again. And as Kitty was about to discover, those winds still blew to the west.

A FORTUITOUS TRIP

In the summer of 1958, a childhood friend of Mary's, Sissy Payne, was preparing to join a Catholic convent in California. Before the long period of initiation required of nuns, Sissy invited Mary out for a visit. Although she was hesitant to leave Kitty, Mary accepted Sissy's offer. Shortly after Mary's arrival at the Payne's four-family apartment near Lexington and Vermont Avenues in Los Angeles, Sissy took Mary on a long trip up and down the coast of California. It was like nothing Mary had ever seen... an endless panorama of lush orange groves, sprawling vineyards, tranquil beaches, and imperial mountains. What struck Mary even more than the glorious California landscape was the stark contrast of Los Angeles to her life back home in the Bronx. While the Bronx literally closed in on the McInerneys, Los Angeles expanded outward into a seemingly limitless horizon.

The wheels that began turning in Mary McInerney the day she stood up to her abusive father a decade ago were now fully churning. What Mary discovered on the coast of California in 1958 would not only change the fate of her family, it was rapidly morphing the landscape of the country, hemorrhaging a great metropolis and transforming what was once a desert of scant missions and cattle ranches into one of the most abundant and iconic places on earth.

Even after the gold rush had transformed San Francisco into a major American city almost overnight, Los Angeles of 1850 was still a tiny pueblo of

1600 residents, mostly ranchers, Native Americans farmers and descendants of Spanish settlers. As the gold rush Yankees gradually spilled into Los Angeles looking to spend their newfound riches, Los Angeles became a place of ill-repute, overrun with prostitution, gambling, thieves, con men, drifters and murderers.

The modest ranching industry in Los Angeles boomed during the gold rush, as hide and beef demand prompted cow prices to inflate fifty times their previous value. But in the early 1860s, a catastrophic flood was followed by two years of extreme drought, nearly destroying the cattle industry. Land prices plummeted and economic despair set in. As the Civil War came to an end in 1865, however, speculators bought up chunks of cheap land, new sources of water were discovered, and a railroad was built connecting Los Angeles to the southern seaport of San Pedro. Agriculture—primarily orange groves—replaced cattle ranching as the city's main industry, luring tens of thousands of new residents to Los Angeles, increasing the population to 100,000 by 1900.

During the first decade of the twentieth century, a series of discoveries and inventions changed Los Angeles forever.

The airplane was invented in 1903. A number of pioneers started building planes in Southern California. When the U.S. entered World War I, airplane orders peaked, and a new industry was borne. By World War II, Los Angeles aircraft plants would employ a quarter of a million people.

Oil had been discovered in the California desert in the late nineteenth century, and oil wells were drilling all across the state by the early 1900s. As the automobile fast became the centerpiece of American life and culture, the oil boom attracted a new wave of migrants seeking overnight wealth. Within two decades, California was producing 20% of the world's oil, most from the Los Angeles Basin.

By 1902, a new art form was emerging from the nickelodeons and starting to gain traction in theaters around the world. Motion pictures were gradually becoming big business, and the few companies that largely controlled the industry were bent on monopolizing the profits. So a wave of fledgling filmmakers made their way west to avoid exorbitant equipment taxes and film stock royalties. Also attracted to the temperate year-round Southern California weather, men like Samuel Goldwyn and Cecil B. DeMille set up shop in Hollywood, a meager village west of Los Angeles. In only a few years, motion pictures became the biggest industry in Los Angeles—the fifth largest in the entire United States. By 1926, Hollywood accounted for 90% of the world's film production.

With industry expanding, the population of Los Angeles tripled to 300,000 in the first decade of the twentieth century, mostly middle-class Protestant migrants from farms and towns in the Midwest, as well as Mexican immigrants who came to work on farms, railroads and in the new factories.

The growing industry and population of Los Angeles meant greater demand for resources. William Mulholland, a water-services engineer, led an underhanded effort by the city of Los Angeles to siphon water from the Owens Valley River. His team constructed a 233-mile aqueduct—completed in 1913—that supplied over 75% of the water to Los Angeles, fueling the city's expanding population and setting off a water controversy that would haunt Los Angeles throughout its history.

Led by motion pictures, aircraft, oil and agriculture, Los Angeles rode a wave of economic booms and busts through the first half of the twentieth century, fighting through the Great Depression and soaring through the Second World War. By the late 1940s, as urban renewal began to ravage New York City, a profound migration started to take hold, vaulting Los Angeles and the State of California to a prominence greater than any oil boom or gold rush.

In the 1950s, New York City declined in population for the first time in the nation's history. A city that had seen massive growth for a century and a half was suddenly contracting, a symptom of the anti-urban vision of leaders like Robert Moses. New York's loss was inevitably someone else's gain. In the two decades that followed World War II, hundreds of thousands of New York residents fled the city in favor of suburban life in nearby New Jersey and Connecticut, or down to the warmer climate of Florida. Even more remarkable, half a million New Yorkers made the three-thousand mile trek across Middle America to take residence in the Golden State, and in particular Los Angeles. New York City would not regain its peak population of the early 1950s until the end of the century. Meanwhile, California's population grew by 50% in the decade of the '50s, surpassing New York as the most populous state in the country by 1962.

Los Angeles, a pueblo of 1600 residents in 1850, had grown to a metropolis of two million people in one century. It gained another half million residents in the 1950s alone. As the people of New York flocked west, so did its culture. In 1957, two Major League Baseball franchises, The Brooklyn Dodgers and New York Giants, announced their moves to Los Angeles and San Francisco, respectively. The end of baseball's Golden Era in New York represented a profound shift of the nation's cultural center from New York to Los Angeles.

Ironically, Los Angeles was no less resistant to the poison of urban renewal than New York. These same forces were fast spreading across America and had taken hold in Los Angeles, spurning pedestrians in favor of automobiles, ripping apart urban neighborhoods to pave room for freeways, packing the poor and underclass into squalid, forgotten quarters of the city, and sprawling the white masses outward into a kind of suburban secession. Los Angeles was as guilty as New York in embracing urban renewal, and it paid a similar price in the currency of poverty, crime, class disparity and racial segregation.

Yet Los Angeles of the mid twentieth century had a few key advantages over New York. Los Angeles had land, and plenty of it, to accommodate suburban expansion. Even in the city, homes and yards were much bigger and offered more privacy. Industry in Los Angeles was booming. Jobs were plentiful. And of course there was the California weather.

As Mary McInerney boarded a plane back to New York, she was touched by everything she had experienced during her two weeks in California. Taking one last step through the aircraft door, Mary heard the desperate shout of Sissy Payne's mother, Margaret, a longtime friend of Kitty's who had fled the Bronx years before. "Jesus, you can do it," she pled. "Bring the family."

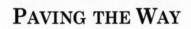

PAVING THE WAY

With the seeds of California planted, Mary McInerney began saving what money she could from her job at Chicago Beef in the Bronx. Yet she was still not completely sure about making the cross-country move. Only after the family moved to the cockroach-infested apartment at Walton Avenue in 1959 did Mary decide the time was right. She approached Kitty first. By this point, Kitty depended so much on Mary that she raised little objection. Mary then paid regular visits to Helen and her husband, George, showing them magazines and whatever materials she could find—"propaganda" as she called it—to try to convince them to make the move too. In time, most of the McInerneys agreed to Mary's plan. A family that had never been farther west than New Jersey was about to take a three-thousand mile journey to an unfamiliar home in Los Angeles.

It was decided that Mary and her younger sister, Margaret, would make the trip first in May of 1960. Mary had managed to save nine-hundred dollars for the move. As the women prepared to make their way to the train station, Kitty fought off tears, seemingly unable to let go of Mary's hand. Knowing how challenging life in the Bronx would be without Mary, Kitty pled for her to come back if anything went wrong. With that, Mary and Margaret said goodbye to their mother and left their Bronx home for the last time.

On May 19th, 1960, the McInerney sisters arrived at Union Station in Los Angeles. They took up temporary residence at the YWCA in the Hayward Hotel downtown. It was a rough start. Margaret missed the family terribly and wanted to go back. Mary countered, arguing that she hadn't even had a chance "to take St. Joseph out of the trunk."

As the days passed, tensions eased. Margaret got a job with Shell Oil while Mary got hired at a customs broker, W.J. Byrnes. Within a couple of weeks, they got an apartment on Bonnie Brae Street in the Mid-Wilshire district of Los Angeles, followed two months later by a move to 11th Street. Helen and her family joined them there a short time later, followed by Paddy and then a fifteen year-old Gerry, who was preparing to start at a new high school.

As the time approached for Kitty and the children to rejoin the rest of the family out west, sadness overtook the family. John's wife, Ida, contracted kidney disease and became gravely ill. Kitty was very fond of her eldest son's kind, generous young wife, as was everyone else in the family. Kitty gathered her children around the Walton apartment to pray for her. On July 13, 1960, Kitty accompanied John to the hospital, but they arrived minutes too late. Ida had succumbed to her illness and died at the age of twenty-six. She left behind a husband and two young daughters.

Any optimism over the imminent move to California was immediately darkened. Kitty was distraught. Adding to her deep sadness over Ida's death, Kitty suffered terribly from her decade-old leg injury that had never properly healed. The monumental task of moving twelve children across the country began to set in. Prior to Helen moving, Kitty quietly revealed to her, "I could go jump in the river." Despite the mounting pressure, Kitty urged Mary to remain in California after Ida's death. Notwithstanding the pain and sadness, Kitty was ready to say goodbye to New York.

I Thought I'd Never See You Again

As winter descended in December of 1960, Kitty McInerney made final preparations for the move to Los Angeles. Mary sent back all the money Margaret and she had saved, but it was still not enough to pay for the move. Eileen's husband, Joe Castrorao, received fifteen hundred dollars in a settlement after being hit by a car and generously lent five hundred to Kitty. The trip was finalized.

The night before the move, Eileen paid a final visit to her mother. Much to her surprise, Kitty's thoughts were not centered on the move or her children's future out west, but on the man she was leaving behind. From the very beginning, Michael McInerney objected to the idea of moving to California. He called it "The Jungle" and thought moving there was crazy. At the same time, he relished the thought of his independence from Kitty and his children.

For the last decade, as Mary asserted herself and the other children got older, Michael's influence over the McInerney household weakened. But his alcoholism continued to spark episodes of brutal conflict. He set off a terrible argument and fist fight on Christmas Day, 1954, after it was revealed he had been hording over seven-hundred dollars in cash. At Theresa's wedding in 1956, he started a brawl with the groom's father. He made his first trip back to Ireland in 1959, only to go on a drunken bender and come back home broken and penniless.

In late 1956, Michael was diagnosed with cirrhosis of the liver. By this point, he had already lost numerous friends to alcoholism-related deaths.   Chris O'Shaunessey was a kind and gentle friend of Michael's whom Kitty had taken care of many times after drunken binges. One morning as Anna walked to the subway, she discovered Chris' lifeless body lying on a bed of rocks. He had gotten drunk and was hit by a car.

Despite cirrhosis and the loss of his closest friends, Michael continued to drink. Yet, somehow, through all the chaos, Kitty maintained a soft place in her heart for her husband. Michael's charm and alluring sense of humor always seemed to mitigate his outrageous behavior, at least with Kitty. So even at the prospect of being liberated from Michael's affliction, Kitty mourned the thought of leaving him behind.

The following morning, as concerns about Michael swirled in her mind, Kitty and twelve of her children set off out of Grand Central Station in the December snow. The train ride from 42nd Street through the outer suburbs offered Kitty one last view of the city that had been her home for the last thirty-five years. When there was no future, New York gave her new life. When there was no family, New York gave her a husband and seventeen children. When there was nothing left to give, New York gave her a train ride to a new place of hope.

Kitty made one brief stop in Buffalo to bid farewell to her daughter Anna. After a tearful goodbye, Kitty and the children set off through a country they'd only imagined. For the first time in three decades, Kitty was able to rest, allowing her leg to finally heal after more than a decade of pain. Throughout the trip, she remained quiet, peaceful. As three thousand miles of the American mainland drifted past her window, Kitty withdrew from the rigors of endless labor and reflected back on her life.

Kitty knew her struggle was not over. California would present many challenges. For a time, twenty-two members of the family would live under one roof. But Kitty knew that through faith, family, and the goodness of others, tomorrow would always be a better day.

On December 7th, 1960, Kitty and her children arrived in Los Angeles to ninety-degree weather—winter in LA. Getting off the train at Union Station, the children gathered around the garden while Kitty grabbed Bonnie and danced to the music playing over the PA. As Mary arrived to greet the family she hadn't seen in seven long months, Kitty was overcome, relieved, exclaiming "I thought I'd never see you again."

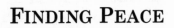

FINDING PEACE

Throughout the decade of the 1960s, circumstances gradually improved for the McInerney clan. Their cramped railroad-style flat in the Bronx was replaced by spacious rental homes west of downtown Los Angeles on Valencia Street and Hobart Boulevard.

As the children got older, the household grew smaller, and with fewer demands at home Kitty was able to earn extra money working a cleaning job at The Tidings Catholic newspaper. In time, Kitty's seventeen children grew up, started their own families, and flourished throughout California and across the country.

In 1975, shortly after her youngest child, Kevin, entered adulthood, Kitty returned for a visit to Scotshouse, County Monaghan, Ireland, some fifty years after setting sail off the coast of Derry. Kitty's mother, father and grandparents were long gone, but she was finally able to reunite with many of her brothers and sisters whom she hasn't seen since they were children.

The husband Kitty said goodbye to in December of 1960 spent a couple of years embarking on drunken binges and living for a time on the streets. He made one unsuccessful attempt to join the family in Los Angeles, but was derailed by another alcoholic episode. Finally, after a couple of years of disastrous independence, Michael McInerney appeared at Kitty's doorstep. A deflated Mary asked him how he got there. His only response: "The bus."

Michael ultimately stopped the binges that characterized his life in New York. Gone were the old bars and old drinking buddies, and Michael could no longer handle the abuse to his body, undoubtedly a result of his cirrhosis. Kitty stuck with Michael till the end, even if his humor and charm eventually wore on her. On a spring evening in 1985, a large chunk of food lodged in Michael's throat. He was taken to the hospital and given a probe, which tore his esophagus. Just before being rushed into emergency surgery, Michael seized a final moment of reflection. After nearly eighty years of self-imposed torment, Michael had a rare moment of clarity about the real presence of beauty in his life. He turned one last time toward Kitty, struggling to give voice to his words. "You were very good to me." Michael McInerney died on April 15th, 1985.

Kitty McInerney spent the last thirty years of her life in a three-bedroom home on Woodbridge Street in North Hollywood. In her latter years, she found her greatest peace passing the days as when she was a young girl roaming the farm in Knocks... cuddling with a dog or cat, picking fruit from the garden, and planting geranium clippings anywhere she could find an empty pot or a small plot of land.

In the early hours of August 30th, 2002, Kitty McInerney passed away at the age of ninety-four, with her daughter, Mary, who had never strayed more than a few blocks away, at her side. Kitty lived long enough to welcome into the world seventeen children, forty-five grandchildren, forty-eight great-grandchildren, and two great-great-grandchildren—one-hundred twelve people who owe their lives to a seventeen year-old girl who left the only family she'd ever known, sailed thousands of miles to a place she'd never been, and created a life and a family out of nothing.

Kitty's life is a testament to the courage of pursuing a better life, the grace of accepting sacrifice, and the generosity of family and community. Kitty McInerney is one small, yet enduring portrait of everyone who has sailed oceans, crossed mountains or journeyed through deserts to forge the hopeful and boundless experience we know as America.

~

BIBLIOGRAPHY

Burns, Margaret. Telephone conversation with author, 2005.

Cadden, Anne. Interviewed by author at her home, County Monaghan, Ireland, 2006.

Caro, Robert A.: *The Power Broker: Robert Moses and the fall of New York. Knopf Publishing; 1974*

Castrorao, Eileen. Interviewed by author at her home, West Covina, CA, 2005.

Coray, Anna. Telephone conversation with author, 2005.

DeMarco, Gordon: *A Short History of Los Angeles.* Lexikos Publishing; 1998.

Gainey, Theresa. Interviewed by author at her home, Santa Anna, CA, 2005.

Hollis, Daniel Webster III: *The History of Ireland.* Greenwood Press; 2001.

Jonnes, Jill: *We're Still Here; The Rise, Fall, and Resurrection of the South Bronx.* The Atlantic Monthly Press; 1986.

Jones, Bernadette. Interviewed by author at her home, Cincinnati, OH, 2005.

Langton, Mary. Interviewed by author at her home, North Hollywood, CA, 2005.

McInerney, Catherine. Tape recorded interview by Gerard McInerney at her home, North Hollywood, CA, circa 1995.

McInerney, Eugene. Interviewed by author at his home, North Hollywood, CA, 2005.

McInerney, Gerard. Interviewed by author at his home, Santa Rosa, CA, 2005.

McInerney, Gerardine. Interviewed by author at Mary Langton's home, North Hollywood, CA, 2005.

McInerney, James. Interviewed by author at his home, San Francisco, CA, 2005.

McInerney, Kevin. Interviewed by author near his home, Santa Rosa, CA, 2005.

McInerney, Patrick. Interviewed by author on airline flight, 2005.

O'Grady, Joseph P.: *How the Irish Became Americans*. Twayne Publishers, Inc.; 1973.

Payne, John. Interviewed by author near his home, New York, NY, 2005.

Prince, Ginny. Interviewed by author at her home, Cincinnati, OH, 2005.

Townshend, Charles: *Ireland: The 20th Century*. Arnold Publishing; 1998.

Vaughan, Helen. Interviewed by author at her home, San Dimas, CA, 2005.

Christopher Prince is a writer and producer in Los Angeles, California, and is proud to be one of Kitty McInerney's forty-five grandchildren. Christopher earned a Bachelor of Fine Arts with highest honors from the University of Cincinnati's Electronic Media Division and a Master of Arts in Film from the University of New Orleans. He has worked in film and television production as a writer, producer and production manager and in interactive marketing as a copywriter, creative project manager, and interactive producer. Christopher always cherished his early childhood memories of Kitty before his family moved away from Los Angeles. Having returned to Los Angeles after graduate school, he feels blessed to have gotten close to Kitty over the last eight years of her life. This book was written in preparation for a feature documentary Christopher is presently producing about Kitty McInerney.